AF337279

Shameless Gasoline Windfalls

Investigation into a Total Scandal

Thomas Porcher

SHAMELESS GASOLINE WINDFALLS

Investigation into a Total Scandal

Max Milo Éditions
Collection Essais-Documents, Paris, 2023
www.maxmilo.com
ISBN : 978-2-31501-232-9

Introduction

At a time when the country is going through a serious economic crisis coupled with a debt crisis, and when the government has announced a second austerity plan that will save eight billion euros, Total is threatening direct and indirect jobs in the refining sector by failing to make the investments needed to maintain the sector's productivity, nibbles away at additional margins on the backs of consumers by failing to pass on oil price movements at the pump fairly, and finally does not contribute to the national effort to emerge from the crisis by not paying income tax in France.

This short book has been written to denounce these indecent practices and to make them known to the general public, because it is through collective denunciation and vigilance that we will force governments to take the necessary measures to oblige companies to behave more fairly towards the inhabitants of producing countries, towards consumers in France and elsewhere, and towards the states in which they operate. We will use the example of Total, a controversial major oil company.

Ever since Total's profits topped the €10 billion mark in 2005, they have been eagerly awaited by French observers, experts and politicians, who have reacted with either admiration or indignation. The debates always revolve around the same question: should Total be ashamed of its profits? My answer is yes.

However, I'm not one of those who think that profits in the billions in the context of a crisis are indecent. Positive results for a French company are normally good news for the country's economy, provided they create jobs, contribute to economic growth in France and help reduce public debt thanks to the tax revenues they generate.

Nor am I shocked by the economic windfall enjoyed by Total: high oil prices for the past eight years. In fact, 2011 was an exceptionally good year for oil companies. Thanks to the Arab revolts, which raised doubts about oil supply against a backdrop of demand driven by growth in emerging countries, prices rose to levels reminiscent of 2008, when crude reached a record $148. Even Europe's debt crisis failed to bring prices below $100 a barrel for very long. A price impossible for Total to imagine just 10 years ago, when the highest forecasts for the next 20 years were barely above $25 a barrel[1]. What salesman wouldn't dream of selling the same product for four times as much? Total, like all oil companies, has benefited from a favorable economic climate since 2004.

But from the extraction of crude oil to the distribution of petrol, there are also indecent practices that enable oil companies to make a few billion on the backs of people in producing countries and consumers around the world.

---

1. In 2000, the cost forecasts of the POLES and WEO 2000 models "with" and "without" Kyoto were fairly close on average over the next 20 years, with a price of around $24 per barrel. These figures have been confirmed in several studies led by oil companies, notably Shell, which has a slightly lower estimate of $20 per barrel.

This book brings these practices to light through eight profit-related controversies. Of course, many of these practices are not unique to Total, but to all oil companies. Some will even tell you that they are necessary, because you have to fight your rivals on equal terms: without these immoral practices, Total would not be able to keep up, and its competitors would end up eating it. They will add that holding Total to account is the best way to drive it abroad. But to what extent can the desire for profit justify non-transparency, collusion to the detriment of a country's inhabitants, the closure of refineries, disloyalty to consumers and the inhabitants of its home base? For many, to reject these practices and want to constrain companies is to be a soft dreamer. I think it's more like facing reality. This book is not a work of fiction; every practice revealed is the result of scientific research backed up by concrete examples.

Admittedly, the ambition is great, and I don't pretend to be able to answer all the questions exhaustively. But time is of the essence, and our approach, combining scientific research findings and concrete examples, is sufficiently accurate to denounce practices that are no longer acceptable in the 21st century, where the need for equitable sharing is now a condition of human survival.

Controversy 1 presents the economic windfall *via* "price effects" enjoyed by all oil companies since 2004.

Controversies 2 to 4 focus on the practices of oil companies in France in gasoline distribution, refining and taxation.

Finally, controversies 5 to 8 concern the practices of oil companies in exploration and production. Many examples focus on the Republic of Congo. There are two reasons for this choice. Firstly, Total is the incumbent operator in the Congo, accounting for 60% of oil production. Secondly, Congo has all the characteristics of a resource-rich, economically poor country. It's important to note that today, half of the world's poor[2] live in an oil-producing country: so the question of oil revenues financing the fight against poverty should have been obvious. But corruption and company practices prevent the efficient use of oil revenues.

----

2. Individual living on less than a dollar a day.

1st Controversy:

Oil Company Profits Driven more by Higher Oil Prices than by Increased Production

"We've got good results because we've worked hard. We can be proud."
Christophe de Margerie

Since 2004, oil company profits have been rising sharply. For many industries, year-on-year increases in profits are the result of improved productivity, leading to lower prices and higher quantities sold. This is not the case for the oil industry. The billions of euros in profits are primarily the result of price effects due to higher oil prices. A price effect is when a company sells the same quantity of a good, but at a higher price. In many industries, it is the producer who decides to raise the price of these products, while taking the risk of seeing demand fall. In the oil industry, it's not the companies that determine prices, but the global confrontation of oil supply and demand, and speculation. They are therefore *"price takers"*, i.e. they receive the price without being able to exercise any individual power on the market. As for price-dependent demand for oil, it is inelastic, i.e. rising prices do not lead to falling demand. In recent years, demand has even risen in line with prices. This peculiarity of the oil industry has enabled companies to benefit fully from the rise in oil prices since 2004. In fact, the world's top 20 multinational corporations include eight oil companies. This is the most represented sector, the second being the automotive industry, with only three companies ranked.

You only have to look at Total's profits over the last three years to understand the power of the price effect. In 2008, Total made a profit of 13.9 billion euros, up 14% on the previous year. Oil prices had risen by 34%, averaging $97 a barrel. Total became France's leading company. A year later, in the midst of the crisis, the average price of oil dropped from $97 to $61 a barrel, and profits fell by 44% to just 7.8 billion euros. Total lost its number-one ranking. The following year, oil prices began to rise again, averaging $79.5 a barrel: Total's earnings rose by 32% to 10.3 billion euros. Oil company profits therefore depend more on price effects than on production growth. In fact, Total revised its average production forecast for 2007-2016 downwards, from 4% to around 2%. It has also announced that it will maintain its production between 2010 and 2011.

But a closer look reveals that these results were unhoped-for just 10 years ago. According to the IEA's 2000 oil price forecasts (WEO 2000), oil prices should have continued to rise, reaching $24 in 2010 and $28 in 2020! If the IEA's forecast had come true, Total would never have posted profits in excess of 10 billion euros. The company has therefore benefited fully from the global economic situation, thanks to rising growth in emerging countries such as China and India. The money generated by price effects is a "windfall" that Total could have invested in the refining sector, which had been under-invested since the 1990s. Unfortunately, this was not the case. In 2010, Total returned five billion euros to its shareholders and paid zero euros in income tax in France.

Conclusion/Action: It's not Total's profits that are indecent, but the way they were obtained. Total is taking advantage of an economic windfall that has multiplied its profits even though its production has increased little or not at all. This is true, because the price of a barrel is largely determined by OPEC, global demand (particularly American and Chinese) and speculation. Total is not involved in any of these three factors. In fact, the price of oil is high because demand is rising, and OPEC sets its production quotas so that supply and demand adjust, leading to price pressure and speculation. However, the very nature of industries selling a product whose value is determined by the global market is that they can both win and lose, without having any control over the factors that lead to this situation. It was this high degree of uncertainty in oil company profits that made politicians reluctant to raise taxes. But today, everyone (oil companies, financial experts, producing countries) agrees that the price of oil can no longer fall sharply. Moreover, the structure of the current market prevents it from remaining low when it has been high for some time[3]. The risk of a sharp drop in oil prices has therefore been averted, and prices will never be the same as in the early 2000s (around $20). Over the next 10 years, oil prices will rise, automatically boosting company profits. At the same time, governments are undergoing a major debt crisis, coupled with an economic crisis. Politicians therefore need to reach agreement at European, or even global, level, to introduce legislation specific to oil companies, enabling them to tax their profits above a certain level. These taxes will have to be shared with producer countries, so that extraction zones (Africa, South America, etc.) benefit as much as consumption zones (Europe, USA, etc.).

---

3. See PORCHER (Thomas), "Crise et prix du pétrole : une baisse pourrait cacher une hausse", L'Expansion.com, 2011.

2ND CONTROVERSY:

OIL COMPANIES ADD MORE PROFITS ON THE BACKS OF CONSUMERS

> "If we don't pass on the rise in oil prices, the company will sink."
>
> "The French retail market is hyper-competitive, with some of the lowest margins in Europe."
>
> Christophe de Margerie

Oil companies, notably Total, have made a commitment to the government to pass on variations in the price of a barrel of oil at the pump, in other words, both increases and decreases. To check that they were living up to their commitments, Mrs Lagarde, then Minister of the Economy, Finance and Industry, commissioned a report from the DGCCRF (Direction Générale de la Concurrence de la Consommation et de la Répression des Fraudes).

The DGCCRF report, presented on May 27, 2011, showed that "the gross transport-distribution margin of the various players had not remained stable, as would theoretically have been the case if crude oil prices had been passed on perfectly and instantaneously", but that between May 2 and 15, it had risen by 3.9 euro cents per liter for SP95 and 2.6 cents for diesel, while the price of oil was falling by 8.5%. However, two months later, in an interview, Christophe de Margerie stated that it was "less than one centime per liter"[4].

On July 8, 2011, another study by four economists from ESG Research Lab[5] analyzed the trajectory of gasoline and crude oil prices over 20 years, to show how oil price trends have been reflected at the pump. Their conclusions concur with those of the DGCCRF, and show that fuel

---

4. "Margerie explains Total's profits", Le Figaro.fr, July 29, 2011.
5. LAMOTTE (Olivier), SHALCK (Christophe), PORCHER (Thomas) and SILVESTRE (Stephan), *Étude sur la répercussion à la pompe des variations du prix du pétrole brut : le cas de la France (1990-2011)*, ESG Research Lab, 2011.

prices adjust upwards as well as downwards, but that the adjustment is weaker in the case of a fall in crude oil prices. For example, the study estimates that a 1% rise in the price of crude oil in euros implies an immediate rise of 0.12% for diesel and 0.08% for SP95, while a 1% fall implies an immediate fall of 0.07% for diesel and 0.05% for SP95, confirming an asymmetry in the response of fuel prices to changes in the price of Brent crude oil. The result is a loss of purchasing power for consumers and a gain for oil companies. Other studies have reached the same conclusions[6], notably a study by INSEE in 2002. Whether short or long term, both reports came to the same conclusion: oil companies take advantage of movements in

6. AUDENIS (Cédric), BISCOURP (Pierre), RIEDINGER (Nicolas), "Le prix des carburants est plus sensible à une hausse qu'à une baisse du brut", *Économie et statistique*, INSEE, vol. CCCLIX, 2002.
GRASSO (Margherita) and MANERA (Matteo), "Asymmetric error correction models for the oil-gasoline price relationship", *Energy Policy*, 2007.
GALEOTTI (Marzio), LANZA (Alessandro), MANERA (Matteo), "Rockets and feathers revisited: an international comparison on European gasoline markets", *Energy Economics*, n° 25, 2003.
BALABANOFF (Stefan), "The composite barrel of retail prices and its relationship to crude oil prices", *OPEC Review*, 1993.

crude oil prices to make additional margins on the backs of consumers.

Two days after the report was published, and in the middle of the vacation weekend for millions of French people, Christophe de Margerie announced an increase in the price of petrol, reminding the French that "we'll have to get used to it" and that "if we don't pass on the rise in the price of a barrel, the company will sink"[7]. The reports accusing the oil companies, combined with Total's statements, rekindled the controversy over the companies' profits, with political recuperation on both the left and the right.

Christophe de Margerie and UFIP President[8], Jean-Louis Schilansky, may have loudly proclaimed that "the distribution market in France is hyper-competitive"[9], but the controversy never subsided. After all, the reports only served to scientifically justify what everyone else had noticed, or rather, had experienced: there is no competition in the French fuel distribution market.

---

7. "Essence en hausse : 'il va falloir s'y habituer'", *France-Soir*, July 11, 2011.
8. UFIP: Union Française des Industries Pétrolières.
9. "Margerie explains Total's profits", Le Figaro.fr, July 29, 2011.

Just look at the figures. Of the 12,000 service stations in France, Total has the biggest market share, with 40%, followed far behind by Carrefour with 10.3%. Among oil companies (producers from upstream to downstream), Total has a virtual monopoly. Second in market share is Esso with 5.8% of stations, followed by BP with 3.3%. Such a market structure is far from "hyper-competitive": there is a "leader", Total, who sets the prices, and the others, the "followers", who position themselves according to Total. In fact, doesn't Christophe de Margerie behave like a leader when he announces increases and decreases in petrol prices?

To put an end to the controversy, Éric Besson, the French Minister for Industry, Energy and the Digital Economy, commissioned a study of how gasoline prices are passed on. The results were published on July 20. For the Minister, the results were "clear": "Total had passed on the fall in oil prices as quickly as the rise", adding that all French distributors had followed the same trend[10]. Our Minister knows

---

10. "Éric Besson: 'Les baisses du prix du carburant ont été répercutées aussi vite que les hausses'", *Le Point,* July 19, 2011.

full well that the market is not competitive, which is why he always distinguishes between Total and "other oil companies". As far as the report is concerned, there is much to criticize in terms of its scientific value. The Minister presented us with a report covering the last six months. But in reality, the study is based on three short periods of the last six months. Any first-year economics student knows that the choice of short periods can influence the results. What's more, the method used by the Minister's office "smoothes" the data, i.e. they do not take into account variations in sub-periods. In the end, they retain only the first and last data of the chosen period. With this type of method, you can make them say anything. It's a bit as if, to prove that the weather was fine in July, all you had to do was choose a day when the weather was good, then find another and conclude: "the weather was fine all July", when it's possible that between the two dates chosen there were only rainy days. This is not a statistically valid conclusion; but then, this report was probably written in a hurry and was not intended to analyze the impact of petroleum product prices, as its title suggests.

Finally, on November 29, 2011, a third study by the association Consommation, logement et cadre de vie (CLCV) came to the same conclusions as the DGCCRF and ESG Research Lab, denouncing the increase in oil company margins over the past 10 years[11].

But even if companies decided to pass on oil price rises and falls just as equitably, the real problem lies in reaction times. A delay of just a few days means millions of euros in extra margins for the oil companies. Margins eaten away from consumers' purchasing power.

Given that the average French person consumes 2.26 liters of gasoline per day (0.5 liters of premium and 1.7 liters of diesel[12]), a margin of one euro cent per liter on additional gasoline (diesel and premium) generates an additional 1.4 million euros per day for oil companies. Using the results of the DGCCRF, this amounts to 4.1 million euros per day, which, over the 13-day study period, comes to more than 53 million euros!

---

11. "Prix des carburants : la faute aux marges des pétroliers", *La Tribune*, November 29, 2011.
12. UFIP.

Oil Companies add more Profits on the Backs of Consumers

Conclusion/Action: Be vigilant! Because, as we've seen, the oil market is far from competitive, and every cent nibbled away means several hundred thousand euros for Total at the end of the day. Conversely, for French households, the share of the budget allocated to petrol is only increasing. It represents 150 euros per month. For a modest household, this is enormous. Vigilance therefore lies in the collective denunciation of certain practices by companies which respect neither their commitments to consumers, nor their commitments to the government, which will only agree to take the necessary measures under pressure from consumers and citizens.

3RD CONTROVERSY:

HOW COMPANIES SCUTTLE THEIR OWN REFINERIES

> "We can't rule out further refinery closures in the next three to five years, perhaps one or two."
> Jean-Louis Schilansky, President of UFIP
> "The need for adaptation [in refining] is unavoidable."
>
> Christophe de Margerie

The French refining sector is in crisis. After Total in Dunkirk and Petroplus in Reichstett in 2010, it was LyondellBasell's turn in 2011 to announce the imminent closure of the Berre refinery, for lack of a buyer. Whereas France had 24 refineries in 1970, only 11 remain in operation today, including 10 in mainland

France. The French refining sector is making heavy losses: Total, which owns half of the refineries, is estimated to have lost 900 million euros in 2009, and the sector as a whole more than 1 billion euros.

The losses are explained by the refining sector's significant production overcapacity. On the one hand, French refineries are producing a surplus of petroleum products, while on the other, structural demand is falling, notably due to the production of lighter, less fuel-intensive vehicles. Added to this is the current crisis, which is squeezing demand even further.

Pointing to the lack of competitiveness of French refineries, UFIP (Union Française des Industries Pétrolières) also notes that refining margins fell to a paltry eight euros per tonne in 2011. With the sector making losses, and new refineries in India and the Middle East able to export fuels to European markets, some of France's refineries, according to the UFIP, will have to disappear in order to adapt supply to demand.

But the problem is more complex than it seems: it stems above all from the fact that the refineries' production facilities are ill-suited to French demand. The last investments in production units date back to the seventies and eighties, and were used to produce gasoline. However, since 1994, French demand for diesel has been rising steadily, while demand for gasoline has been falling sharply. Today, demand for diesel accounts for 80% of fuel demand, and France finds itself obliged to export its production, which it is unable to sell domestically, and to import diesel. This is an unusual situation in which the French refining sector, which is designed to ensure security of supply, has production levels that are ill-suited to domestic demand.

The cause of this ridiculous situation lies in the lack of investment in changing the production structure of French refineries. Record profits due to the price effect have been used more to create refineries close to extraction areas than to adapt those in France. In Saudi Arabia, for example, Total has invested in the Jubail refinery, which not only offers low-cost production due to its proximity to the deposits, but is also equipped with a modern system for adapting the desired diesel/petrol ratio. A technology that would be of great use in our country...

How Companies Scuttle their Own Refineries

The argument that refining margins are falling should also be treated with caution. The calculation of the gross refining margin is the difference between the value of refined products (gasoline, diesel, etc.) on the Rotterdam market minus the cost of purchasing oil, which includes the price of crude (on the markets), but also freight and insurance. This margin therefore depends more on the volatility of market prices for refined products and crude oil than on the productivity of refiners, who are often held responsible for the sector's losses. If market trends lead to an increase in the spread between the prices of petroleum products and crude oil, then the refining sector makes margins without even changing its real productivity (and vice versa for losses). Just look at the figures for refining gross margins on Brent (euro per tonne) over the last three years to understand the volatility of the sector: the margin averaged 39 euros in 2008, fell to 15 euros in 2009 and then rose to 21 euros in 2010. The monthly figures for 2011 are even more striking, with a margin of 10 euros in June 2011 - justifying for some the low competitiveness of French refineries - whereas a few months earlier, in March, it was 22 euros[13]. It therefore seems clear that French refineries have no control over their margins, which, subject to market volatility, can fluctuate as rapidly as the value of a share on the stock market. But what is shocking is that direct and indirect refinery employees and their families, who have no influence whatsoever on either the Rotterdam market or the crude oil market, are taken hostage by the unfortunate fluctuations of these markets and bear the full risks (refinery closures, job losses, etc.). These people number in the tens of thousands, but some will tell you that this is economic logic.

What's more, this system of margins has not always worked against the oil companies. As noted by IFP[14] (Institut Français du Pétrole), oil companies' financial losses due to falling oil prices can be offset by a moderate fall in gasoline prices. In fact, this is what happened in the fourth quarter of 2008, when the fall in oil prices automatically led to a 37% increase in refining margins.

---

13. Data from UFIP.

14. BAUDOUIN (Colin) and FAVENNEC (Jean-Pierre), *Les Marges de raffinage : évolution récente*, IFP, 1999.

How Companies Scuttle their Own Refineries

Lastly, we need to put refinery losses into perspective. Take Total, for example: the company is said to have lost 900 million euros in refining in 2009. This is a huge figure, but one that will be almost made up if the price of a barrel rises by one euro[15]. It's even more striking when we take into account the price effects from which the companies have benefited: with a barrel averaging $77.5 between 2007 and 2010, while the IEA[16] was forecasting a price of $24 in 2010, the oil companies have generated billions. More than enough to cover the investments needed to restructure French refineries, estimated by the French Petroleum Institute at 2.2 billion euros over 10 years.

The problem facing the French refining industry is therefore more akin to "technical unemployment in the sector", orchestrated by the companies themselves, who have refused to change unsuitable means of production, than to a real problem of competitiveness. Although the former begets the latter.

---

15. Given that Total produces 2.3 million barrels a day, or 854 million barrels a year, an extra euro per barrel of production generates an additional 854 million euros, virtually making up for all the losses of its five refineries.
16. WEO 2000.

Conclusion/Action: As we have pointed out in previous controversies, the higher the price of oil on the crude oil market, the more oil companies are making profits from exploration. But, paradoxically, refineries also appear less profitable. So, the greater the company's exploration profits, the more refineries it wants to close, as stock market logic drives management to satisfy shareholders by selling off the weakest production units. Their survival thus seems to depend above all on the somewhat hazardous movements of spot crude oil markets.

This abandonment to market forces is unacceptable. Maintaining refineries in France is essential, as they ensure security of supply. The alternative of the disappearance of refineries in France could prove dramatic: the country would then be at the mercy of importers who could impose price constraints by themselves influencing the import schedule. French islanders are already familiar with this situation, and periodically demonstrate against its damaging effects.

4TH CONTROVERSY:

OIL COMPANIES PAY NO TAXES IN THEIR OWN COUNTRIES, NOR IN OIL-PRODUCING COUNTRIES.

"It would be totally abnormal and unconstitutional to pay an additional tax in France on money we don't earn."
Christophe de Margerie

While Total made a profit of 10.3 billion euros in 2010, the company paid no income tax in France. This was due to the losses incurred by Total's refineries in France. But the company's CFO, Patrick de la Chevardière, notes that Total pays corporate income tax in every country where the company makes a profit, and adds that, even though it paid zero corporate income tax in France, it contributed some 800 million euros in tax revenue to the country in 2010, through other taxes.

However, even taking into account all types of tax paid by Total, a report by the Conseil des prélèvements obligatoires published in October 2010 showed that CAC 40 companies were taxed at an average of 8% on their profits, compared with 22% for SMEs.

This is because Total benefits from a special regime - the BMC (Bénéfice Mondial Consolidé) regime - granted by the French government, which allows the group to deduct losses incurred abroad from its taxes. However, this regime is advantageous when Total makes losses abroad and profits in France, which is completely the opposite since it loses money in France and makes profits abroad.

However, in July 2011, tired of "hearing all day long that the company benefits from a preferential regime"[17], Total decided to abandon the BMC and apply the territoriality tax regime for income tax purposes.

But in reality, all these changes in tax regimes are more a matter of publicity than a

____

17. Total's Chief Financial Officer, Patrick de la Chevardière.

real citizen's initiative. Total will not be paying more tax next year. Firstly, because by switching from the BMC regime to the territoriality tax regime for income tax, Total will not be taxed on its overall profits, i.e. on the 10.3 billion euros it has already earned. This is because, under Article 209-I of the French General Tax Code (CGI), profits subject to corporation tax are only those earned by companies operating in France. However, "if the income is realized through a structure located abroad, but without a legal personality of its own, the French tax authorities will have to determine whether this entity can be assimilated to a genuine business operating outside France, within the meaning of Article 209-I of the CGI, on a regular basis, or whether it is merely the economic, legal and tax extension of the French company. In the first case, the profits generated by the operation will be taxed in the State where they originate, as if it were a subsidiary. In the second case, such income will be attached to the French company and subject to French corporation tax"[18]. As a result, Total's income tax is likely to

---

18. TOUZET (Claire), MARCHESSOU (Pr), (under the direction of), *La Territorialité de l'impôt sur les sociétés*, DEA Droit des

be zero again next year, as it will only concern the refining and distribution business. And even if part of the profits were consistent with the second case, it is highly likely that Total would change the structure of the entity to transform it into a subsidiary and thus pay its taxes abroad.

But if Total doesn't pay taxes in France, how much does it pay abroad, where its activities are profitable?

Let's take the case of the Congolese tax system. The 1994 law has two components: corporate income tax (IS) and proportional mining royalties. The corporate income tax rate is set at 35% for a period of five years for all operating permits stemming from a single exploration permit. This rate can then be increased to 50%. However, despite extracting tens of millions of barrels a year, Total pays no corporate income tax in the Congo. This is because, when taxes are high in a country, oil companies sell to sister companies and generally use very low transfer prices. In our example, Total's subsidiary in Congo sells the oil cargoes it recovers to a sister company for

---

affaires dissertation, Université Robert Schuman, 2001.

a very low price, enabling it just to balance its expenses. By making virtually no profit, it is therefore unable to pay taxes in Congo. For its part, the sister company, which is registered in a low-tax zone, has obtained oil at a cheap price, which it resells this time at a real price[19] to other companies. In the end, the profit-generating transaction always takes place in a low-tax location. It should be pointed out, however, that the weaker the institutions in producing countries, the more likely it is that this little game of make-believe will work.

And yet, according to Total's CFO, the company's overall tax rate is 56%. But precisely because this figure is provided by the company itself, it depends on the credibility of the administrations of the 130 countries in which the company operates. Credibility which the French authorities are not required to verify. The situation is therefore one of information asymmetry and transparency, akin to the situation of assessing the value of the deposit, which we'll look at in the next controversy.

---

19. In other words, close to the price per barrel.

Conclusion/Action: Increasingly detached from its national base, Total is a global company that manages to avoid excessive taxation, shifting its profits to countries where it can make a profit with lower taxes. Such disloyalty to the governments of producing and wealthy countries is no longer acceptable in the 21st century, at a time when financing the fight against poverty in developing countries has become a Millennium Development Goal, and wealthy countries are going through a serious debt crisis. Citizens, who own the state budget, must put pressure on politicians to change the tax system, because without international coordination of states imposing a common tax system for oil companies, this situation will continue and get worse.

5th Controversy:

Oil Companies Deliberately Undervalue Deposits in Oil-Producing Countries

> "Total needs Africa economically."
> "We are present in virtually every oil-producing country in Africa."
>
> Christophe de Margerie

Most oil-producing countries have neither the technical nor the financial resources to exploit their oil resources. They therefore call on private oil companies to set up exploration and production programs for their deposits.

An oil exploration program always begins with the collection of data (geological, geophysical, etc.), which is then analyzed by company experts to estimate the deposit's chances of success, its probable size and profitability. This information, necessary to establish the value of the deposit, must be supplied to the country holding the interest. But as this information gathering is carried out by the private companies, they are the only ones who know the real value of the country's deposits, on which the bidding and sharing contracts between the country and the company are supposed to be based. It's a strange situation, where the buyer (the company) evaluates the price of a product on behalf of the seller (the country), and then buys it from the seller at the price set by the buyer. The question is whether a well-informed company can have any interest in being transparent, i.e. in communicating accurate information on the value of the deposit to the producing country.

Numerous studies[20], including those by Crawford and Sobel[21], show that if the

---

20. PHLIPS (Louis), *The Economics of Imperfect Information*, Cambridge University Press,1988.HUGHART (David), "Informational asymmetry, bidding strategies, and the marketing of offshore petroleum leases", *Journal of Political Economy*, vol. LXXXIII, 1975.
21. CRAWFORD (Vincent P.) and SOBEL (Joel), "Strategic information transmission", *Econometrica*, 1982.

interests of two agents do not completely coincide, then non-transmission of information is compatible with rational behavior. The rational behavior of a company would therefore be to conceal the true information it holds concerning the deposit and to transmit biased data to the producing states. The aim is to underestimate the value of the deposit, so that the auction price is not too high, and production is shared under conditions that are favorable to the company.

As a result, information becomes scarce, generating rents, because while oil companies are the only ones able to correctly assess the value of deposits, they jealously guard their expertise and know how to profit from it for themselves, to the detriment of the oil-producing country.

A recent World Bank report on Congo's oil revenues underlines this point: "Neither the Ministry of Finance and Budget nor the Ministry of Hydrocarbons has sufficient capacity to forecast production volumes and the level of oil revenues. They therefore rely on data supplied by the oil companies in accordance with contractual requirements. This dependence on the oil companies' production

Oil Companies Deliberately Undervalue Deposits in Oil-Producing Countries

data (estimated production volumes and costs) makes it difficult for the Ministry of Hydrocarbons [...] to evaluate the development proposals for each field made by the companies."[22]

Another report by AFD[23] (Agence Française du Développement) shows that oil companies pass on false estimates to producing countries in order to increase their profits (overestimation of production costs, underestimation of oil quality or reserves, etc.). He adds: "Cheating on production is first and foremost the easiest way for oil companies to defraud."

Several cases demonstrate the manipulation of information by oil companies. One example is the Nkossa platform project, in which the Republic of Congo is participating with oil companies. According to Total, the Nkossa project cost $2 billion, whereas the initial investment had been set at $800 million,

---

22. WORLD BANK, for the Republic of Congo, "Making the most of oil wealth to accelerate and diversify growth", *Public Expenditure Review*, Washington, 2010, p. 124.
23. LEENHARDT (Blaise), AFP, Research Department, Jumbo thematic report, *Production, fiscalité, transparence et gestion des revenus pétroliers en Afrique subsaharienne et en zone franc; la chance des Africains?*, 2004, pp. 22-23.

resulting in a highly suspicious overrun of $1.2 billion. It's important to understand that, although the investment required to bring the field into production is borne solely by the company, it repays the amount invested by capturing an additional share of the production. So, the higher the amount invested, the greater the company's share of oil production, to the detriment of the producing country's share. Conversely, for the country, the lower the initial investment, the greater the share of oil production it recovers[24]. In our case, the oil companies presented the Congolese authorities with investment forecasts estimated at 800 million dollars, accompanied by simulations of the share of production that would revert to the Congo under these conditions. Unable in any case to verify the relevance of the information provided by the companies, and with management probably in a hurry to concede, they validated the project, thinking they would recover a predefined amount of production. But once the

---

24. In short, the less investment a field requires, the greater the return to the country, to the detriment of the oil company. Conversely, the more investment a field requires, the greater the return to the company, to the detriment of the country.

Oil Companies Deliberately Undervalue Deposits in Oil-Producing Countries

deposit had been acquired, the companies presented the Congolese authorities with a bill for two billion dollars, mechanically accompanied by a reduction in the share of production that Congo was initially expected to obtain. The oil companies' unique control of information enables them to pull off this kind of sleight of hand, based on a double manipulation of information: 1) to make the producing country believe that it will recover a significant share of production, because the investments required to operate the field are low, 2) once the field has been obtained, to over-invoice the initial investment in order to reappropriate an additional fraction of the share initially due to the country.

In the Nkossa case, an out-of-court settlement avoiding a trial for forgery and accounting manipulation enabled the Congo to receive compensation of nearly $80 million in 2004[25].

But it gets worse. In 1997, Sao Tome and Principe, an archipelago of 180,000 inhabitants located in the Gulf of Guinea, heavily in debt and dependent on international

---

25. A summary report of the negotiations is available on the Internet.

aid, discovered that it possessed, according to company data, oil reserves estimated at 11 billion barrels. Shortly afterwards, it signed an extremely disadvantageous contract with ERHC (Environmental Remediation Holding Corporation), described by observers as the "worst oil contract in history"[26]: even before it produced its first barrel, Sao Tome and Principe had already been deprived of an income of over 60 million dollars, while its annual budget was only 50 million dollars[27]!

Many civil society associations, such as the Observatoire congolais des droits de l'homme and the Conférence épiscopale du Congo in Congo (supported by Secours catholique français, Cimade and Catholic Relief Services), are denouncing the lack of transparency in the management of oil revenues, and are calling on the heads of oil companies (notably Total) to make public the revenues they pay to producing countries.

---

26. "Le pire contrat pétrolier de l'histoire", jeuneafrique.com, December 16, 2008.
27. "Sao Tomé and Nigeria: inquiry finds lack of transparency and serious flaws in oil licensing round", publishwhatyoupay. org, January 16, 2006.

In 2002, growing pressure from civil society and international organizations led to the creation of the Extractive Industries Transparency Initiative (EITI), signed by 26 countries and 40 companies. Its aim is to provide clearer information on extractive industry revenues received by governments[28] and on payments made by multinational companies. The initiative has had some modestly positive repercussions, as transparency in oil management remains far too limited for the time being.

Conclusion/Action: Transparency about the value of oil fields and the payment of oil revenues is a minimum requirement. It enables the citizens of the world, producer countries and certain organizations (national and international NGOs) to monitor the commitments and practices of oil companies. The role of the Extractive Industries Transparency Initiative (EITI) must therefore be expanded,

---

28. The sharing of rents between the state and its citizens is also a problem in Africa. As Rossellini (2005) points out, oil rents in Africa are "monopolized by agents who are members of or close to the State, redistributed privately or *via* clientelist networks... They do not promote transparency and encourage tax evasion".

and it must be staffed by competent experts who can verify, at random or on request, the information used to determine the value of the deposit. Producing countries with little or no experience of oil production will thus be able to benefit from the experience of EITI experts. This increase in transparency will also help to avoid excessive collusion between oil companies and the governments of producing countries, to the detriment of the inhabitants of these countries.

6th Controversy:

Oil Companies Collude to Buy up Deposits More Cheaply

[About new Chinese companies in Africa].
"Our policy is to involve them as much as possible, even if we remain competitors."
"If we have illegal practices, let them take us to court!"

Christophe de Margerie

After exploration, an oil deposit is put up for auction by the producing country. The bid is calculated on the basis of data supplied by the exploration company. The winning bidder is awarded the right to exploit the deposit with the host country. In theory, in this case, oil-producing countries are in a strong position, as they can use competition between companies to extract maximum profit.

But in reality, competition is very limited, because oil companies have no interest in competing. Let's take the example of a car auction. If there are many interested buyers, competition can lead the one who eventually wins to pay a much higher price than the car's real value. In economics, this phenomenon of over-valuation of the auctioned object is known as the "winner's curse"[29].

This phenomenon increases with the number of participants in the auction, because the more competitors there are, the less chance the future winner has of making a profit, and the higher the bid, the greater the risk of loss. Faced with this risk, the aim of the oil companies is to reduce competition to prevent it from being destructive, and to obtain the deposits at an advantageous price. And the best way to do this is to collude.

Collusion is an arrangement between several agents to the detriment of a third party.

---

29. WILSON (Robert), "A bidding model of perfect competition", *Review of Economic Studies*, vol. XLIV, No. 3, 1977.

Here, the third party harmed by the arrangement is the oil-producing country.

Certainly, there are costs involved in organizing and coordinating collusive activities, but they are very small compared to the profits made afterwards. The existence of collusive agreements between companies has been demonstrated by numerous scientific studies, including those by Nyouki, Feinstein, Graham and Marshall or McAfee and McMillan[30].

It should be noted that the smaller the number of companies per country, the greater the possibility of reaching a collusive

---

30. NYOUKI (Évariste), "Asymétries d'informations et stratégies des compagnies dans l'exploration pétrolière", in *Énergie et théorie économique*, Paris, Cujas, 1997.
MCAFEE (R. Preston) and MCMILLAN (John), "Bidding rings", *American Economic Review*, vol. LXXXII, n° 3, 1992.
GRAHAM (Daniel A.) and MARSHALL (Robert C.), "Collusive bidder behavior at single-object second-price and English auctions", *Journal of Political Economy*, vol. XCV, no. 6, 1987.
GRAHAM (Daniel A.), MARSHALL (Robert C.) and RICHARD (Jean-François), "Differential payments within a bidder coalition and the Shapley value", *American Economic Review*, vol. LXXX, n° 3, 1990.
FEINSTEIN (Jonathan S.), BLOCK (Michael K.) and NOLD (Frederick C.), "Asymmetric information and collusive behavior in auction markets", *American Economic Review*, vol. LXXV, No. 3, 1985.

agreement. This is true in most producing countries, where the number of operators is limited and market or production shares per deposit are predefined between them.

Let's take the Congo as an example: Total owns 60% of production, Agip 30% and the rest is shared between several other companies. This means that 90% of Congolese production is held by just two companies. This is also the case in Gabon, where despite the withdrawal of the majors due to declining production from all the fields, Total and Shell still hold over 50% of production in 2010, compared with 90% (as in Congo) 10 years ago, when the fields were operating at full production. With two main operators sharing the majority of a country's production, you'd have to be pretty naive to think that these companies are in fierce competition with each other.

The strategy of collusion between companies often takes the form of sharing the areas to be exploited. As a result, the companies are not really in competition when it comes to allocating deposits, each having its own field of action.

In 2004, the bidding process for the Sao Tomé and Principe oilfields confirmed this strategic approach. Indeed, many oil companies, notably Total, did not even take part in the tender. Why not? Initial exploration results showed an oil production potential on a par with Gabon. Could Total have inadvertently missed this opportunity? Or did the company simply abide by a rule of non-participation in these auctions, in exchange for the future withdrawal of other companies from other auctions in other zones? Total has bought a 45.9% stake in a concession won by Chevron in the Nigeria/Sao Tomé and Principe joint exploitation zone.

In other words, rather than compete and risk driving up the price of the field at auction, Total did not participate in the sale, enabling Chevron to win the field quickly and at a low price. Total then buys back almost half the operating shares. In this kind of arrangement, the big loser is of course the producing country, which sells these deposits below their intrinsic value thanks to the manipulation of information and illicit agreements between the companies. But it's even more appalling when you consider that most oil-producing countries are single-producer countries, highly dependent on oil revenues, especially for food, and home to half the world's poor.

Oil Companies Collude to Buy up Deposits More Cheaply

Whereas in a country with "good governance"[31], it would only take $100 per person per year for 10 years in social investment to lift people out of poverty, it's clear that for the people of the Congo, every dollar counts. This figure is all the more telling when compared with the oil companies' arrangements, which have cost the Congo over 1.5 billion dollars in lost revenue over 20 years[32]. But there will

---

31. In 2005, Sachs estimated the average annual financing needs for social investments made by a country "in good governance" between 2005 and 2015 to lift the populations of developing countries out of poverty, at $100 per person per year. Social investment needs are broken down as follows: 45 dollars for basic infrastructure (roads, investment in soil regeneration, water availability for irrigation, drinking water and sanitation, modern fuels for cooking), 30 dollars for basic health expenditure (fight against tuberculosis and childhood diseases, for safe childbirth, nutrition and family planning), 15 dollars for improving education (primary and secondary courses); finally, other important priorities would entail an additional expenditure of around 10 dollars, bringing the total investment required to 100 dollars per person per year.
32. PORCHER (Thomas), *Un baril de pétrole contre 100 mensonges*, Res Publica, 2009. Negotiations took place between the Congo, Total and partner Agip, concerning the disputes between the Congo and the oil companies in the early 2000s - companies to which the Congo allegedly claimed the sum of three billion dollars.

always be those who argue that, in any case, the Congo is not a country of good governance.

Conclusion/Action: Collusion between companies enables them to buy deposits from producing countries at below their value. These arrangements are often contrary to national laws, but the risk of sanction is low, as developing countries have neither the technical nor the financial means to control oil companies. The famous Elf affair showed just how difficult it was for a country like France to control its own national oil company.

Supervision of the auctions should therefore be carried out by a supranational authority (such as a UN agency), which would itself be auditable and accountable for the way in which the auctions were carried out.

We also need to extend the possibility of taking legal action before an international court to have the fairness of auctions judged. At present, only the parties who took part in the auction, or an unsuccessful competitor, can take legal action against the auction before an international court. Opening up this possibility of recourse to transaction monitoring associations would constitute a first check.

7th Controversy:

Oil Companies do not Share Revenues Equitably with Producing Countries

> "The issue is governance, not oil. In Africa, it's about behavior. And that applies not just to Africans, but to every link in the chain."
>
> "It's no longer a question of knowing what we want and imposing it on them. It's a question of knowing what they want and seeing how we can deliver it."
>
> Christophe de Margerie

The key issue in any oil production agreement is to define how production is to be shared between the state that owns the field and the oil company. Because of the diversity of producing countries, there are different types of contract. The main patrimonial contracts used in the oil industry are concession contracts[33] and production sharing contracts[34]. Today, production contracts are the most commonly used, particularly in sub-Saharan Africa[35] .

In economic terms, the production sharing contract consists of sharing oil production

33. Under the concession system, the State transfers its exploration or production rights to an oil company for a fixed period, which is generally the life of an oil field (20 to 30 years). The company conducts and finances exploration at its own risk. In the event of a discovery, it decides on development and exploitation within the legal framework of the country's mining law, and bears all expenses. Unless otherwise stipulated, the oil company is free to dispose of the production to which it is entitled on the basis of its participation in the development.

34. Under a production sharing contract, the State delegates its rights to explore and exploit the subsoil to an oil company for a fixed period (which is also generally equivalent to the life of a field). The oil company carries out exploration at its own risk, and in the event of a discovery, decides on development and exploitation within the legal framework of the country's mining law, and bears the costs of development and exploitation. The State remains the owner of the hydrocarbons: the company acts only as a contractor, entitled to a share of the production as remuneration for the risks incurred and services rendered.

35. LAMOTTE (Olivier) and PORCHER (Thomas), "Stratégie des compagnies pétrolières internationales et partage de la rente : le cas du Congo", *Management et avenir*, n° 42, 2010.

between the company and the producing country, while deducting the costs of producing the deposit (exploration and exploitation). However, as the company bears the costs, it must deduct from the government's share the part of the cost that the latter would normally have had to bear. This amount is generally paid in barrels of oil.

The State is therefore not involved in oil exploration or production; its role is simply to recover part of the production deducted from the costs incurred by the company. In other words, production is shared between the state, which owns the oilfields, and a private company, which acts as a sort of farmer-operator. However, unlike a farmland owner who has had several successive farmers on the same land, and is therefore familiar with the fertility of his land, the oilfield owner will generally have only one operator, who has had many fields before, and with whom the owner will have to sign a contract for 20 to 30 years (the average life of an oilfield).

This is where the difficulty arises in contract negotiation for the producing country, which is based solely on assumptions about cost levels - assumptions made by the company's experts,

Oil Companies do not Share Revenues Equitably with Producing Countries since, as we've said, they are the ones who have the reservoir's characteristics analyzed and store the information needed for its valuation. Oil rents can be shared according to technical parameters (depth, daily or cumulative production), accounting parameters (price, profitability, surtax) or financial parameters (profitability). Unfortunately, the producing country has no control over any of these parameters.

Moreover, the amount of the costs invested by the company to explore a deposit and the cost of extracting a barrel of oil are not included in the contracts. Instead, they are replaced by the *cost-oil* mechanism: a fixed but variable total cost. It's a simple mechanism that allows companies to make huge profits at the expense of the producing country.

In contracts, the value of *cost oil*, which is supposed to represent the cost of production, is generally set at around 50% of the price per barrel. It may be lower if the exploration concerns an onshore or shallow offshore field. It is generally higher in very deep waters or for newly exploitable fields[36]. In any given

---

36. The high price per barrel makes it possible to profitably exploit deposits in areas that are more difficult to access, or

field, the cost of producing a barrel of oil is therefore a variable cost. However, the barrel contains the same quantity of oil and, for the same deposit, the cost of extraction, excluding the first fixed costs, should be constant. However, the cost of producing a barrel of oil depends more on variations in the price of Brent on the financial markets than on real costs (prospecting, investment, maintenance, wage costs). So, whereas in other industries, cost drives price, in the oil industry, price drives cost.

At company level, the majority of costs are often already invested, and therefore almost entirely known, before the deposit goes into production. The costs that come into play afterwards are platform maintenance and operating costs, which are very low in comparison with previously invested costs (less than 1% of a field's total operating costs). Oil companies could therefore disclose the amount of their investments (the true costs), cover the costs from oil production under equitably established contracts and, once reimbursed,

---

in very deep seas, thus increasing the *cost oil* component of contracts.

Oil Companies do not Share Revenues Equitably with Producing Countries

share the remainder of the oil production fairly with the producing country.

Instead, the companies don't disclose the real costs, and with impunity take 50% of production over the lifetime of the field (around 25 years), even though it has often already paid for itself halfway through its life. Establishing a fictitious, variable *cost oil is by* far the biggest scam perpetrated by oil companies.

It's true that the mechanisms of production sharing contracts mean that the higher the price per barrel, the more money producing countries earn back from production. The rise in oil prices since 2004 has therefore also benefited producer countries and their governments.

However, in the event of a prolonged change in the price per barrel, companies do not hesitate to put pressure on producing countries (which often need financing) to modify legislation and/or contracts, if necessary by relying on local elements and/or existing or potential local political opposition. The recurrent unrest in Chad, Mauritania and other oil-producing countries - especially those without a solid democratic base - is far from independent of the way oil revenues are shared.

In the Congo, while a World Bank report recommends that the government introduce measures to "strengthen the quality of companies' investment and operating cost estimates"[37], companies are lobbying for changes to the terms of production sharing contracts: for example, *cost oil* could rise from 50% to 70% of production, which would considerably reduce the share accruing to the Congo.

Conclusion/Action: Whereas in other industries, cost determines price, in oil production, price determines projected cost. But above all, whereas in other industries, the higher the cost, the lower the profit, in oil production, the higher the conventional cost, the higher the profit. Not only is the *cost oil* paid to oil companies purely conventional, and far exceeds the costs of exploration and exploitation, but it also takes no account of the costs borne by collateral parties to contracts (costs of diminishing reserves for future generations, immediate environmental pollution destroying opportunities for food production, higher prices for everyday consumption, etc.).

------

37. WORLD BANK, *op. cit.* p. 92.

It is therefore necessary to reintegrate these costs into the *cost of oil,* and have them reimbursed to the populations of the oil exploration and/or production regions. This reintegration could take the form of a tax of one dollar per barrel extracted[38], to be reused in the form of a subsidy for the local production of basic necessities, under the supervision of an *ad hoc* committee. The "oil for food" experiment in Iraq, which was supposed to enable the embargoed Iraqi people to exchange some of their oil for humanitarian aid, led to a vast corruption scandal involving French personalities and companies, notably Total. In the end, the program was diverted from its purpose, and this experience reminds us that it's not just good ideas that need to be embraced, but also the committees charged with implementing them.

---

38. In addition to the PID (Provision for Diversified Investments) representing 1% of oil production.

8th Controversy:

How Companies Eat into the Profits of Producing Countries

> "It's not having the best seismic that will set us apart - and of course we'll have the best - but listening, seeing producing countries as partners and helping them build schools, train local staff or promote research."
>
> [About Nigeria's new Petroleum Industry Bill (PIB):]
>
> "I told the president that, in France, GDP means 'gross domestic product', and I told him I hoped that in Nigeria it also meant 'growth'. At least for us..."
>
> Christophe de Margerie

Aside from oil contracts, oil companies have other instruments at their disposal to nibble away at the profits of oil-producing countries. The most widely used are crude oil discounts and pre-sales.

Discounting crude oil means applying a penalty to the oil produced, depending on its quality. In this case, it is the country of extraction that bears the loss resulting from the poor quality of its oil. The companies - which, let's not forget, have the technical expertise and the information - take great pleasure in underestimating the quality of the oil, in order to overestimate the discount and thus appropriate the extracted oil at a lower price and at the expense of the producing countries.

This is exactly what happened in the Congo. The oil companies (Total, Agip, etc.) consider Congolese crude to be of lower quality than the Brent crude they quote. It is therefore priced at a discount to Brent on the international market. This discount varies between 1.5 and 3 dollars, with an average of 2 dollars on the market, according to the companies' claims. However, these claims are not based on market data, since the companies only sell to their sister companies (group subsidiaries) or to the parent company (management) at transfer or accounting prices that impoverish some subsidiaries, particularly where tax pressure is high, and enrich others where taxation is advantageous.

Unable to verify the quality of its crude (Djeno) or the actual existence of a discount, Congo commissioned a market study from an independent firm. The firm concluded that the discount on the crude did not reflect its intrinsic quality, and that Congo should (or should have) recovered one dollar per barrel. In other words, for 2010, $60 million went into the companies' coffers rather than into the Congolese state budget! In other words, a total shortfall of over $650 million over the 25 years of production.

Pre-sale, on the other hand, consists of an oil-producing country selling its production over a quarter or a year at a price fixed in advance. This practice stems from a two-fold dysfunction in oil-producing countries. Firstly, many countries have no control over their production policy, which is set by the private oil company. Admittedly, the company informs the government of its production intentions through a three-year forecast plan for each license area, but the government can only dispose of its oil once the company has

How Companies Eat into the Profits of Producing Countries

decided to extract it. Secondly, oil-producing countries are heavily dependent on oil revenues, which account for 70% to 80% of their budgets, and a large part of the market economy (public services, small-scale commerce, etc.) is directly or indirectly dependent on oil rents. It is this lack of control over oil production and economic dependence on oil that drives countries to sell their oil in pre-sale. For the company buying the oil, the real problem with pre-sales is that the price of a barrel at time T is not necessarily the same as it will be in a month or a year. Its value can go down as well as up. Theoretically, therefore, the company that buys oil a year in advance is taking a risk.

But if we take the Congo as an example, an analysis of the facts shows the opposite to be true. The SNPC (Société Nationale des Pétroles du Congo) pre-sells its oil to companies operating in the country (Total, Agip, etc.) three to nine months in advance. Between 2002 and 2005, SNPC sold more and more, selling almost a year's worth of cargo in advance. At what price did SNPC sell its oil to the oil companies?

The pre-sale value is most often the result of a trade-off between the spot market price (current price per barrel) at the time of negotiation and the price trajectory forecast by the IEA (International Energy Agency)[39] forecasting models, minus an invisible discount (added to the quality discount) to cover the buyer's risk. Because, like any other trader, when oil companies buy large quantities of oil, they ask the producing country for a rebate.

For example, oil pre-sales in 2003 did not reflect the true value of oil on the spot market. At the time of negotiation in December 2002, the spot market price and the IEA model forecast averaged $24. The 85 million Congolese barrels sold in 2003 at a price of $20 (due to a quality discount of $2 and a buyer's risk discount of $2). Did Congo make a bargain? In 2003, the price per barrel on the spot market averaged $29. Congo therefore lost $9 per barrel. In other words, a loss for Congo and a gain for the companies of more than $252 million.

To understand the magnitude of this figure, we need only compare it to the total development aid received by the Congo, i.e. almost $25 million in 2003. In 2003, the Congo lost the equivalent of 10 years' development aid.

---

39. WEO (World Energy Outlook) 2000.

How Companies Eat into the Profits of Producing Countries

The same thing happened in 2004, when, during the summer, the price reached $50 for WTI[40] and $44 for Brent. Nor was Congo able to negotiate pre-sales to match the soaring prices, as the lack of visibility and the inability to forecast market trends fuelled all the uncertainties. The only point of reference in these turbulent times remained the forecasting models and explanations of the experts. At the time, estimates pointed to a price of $24 a barrel, so Congo sold its oil in 2004 once again at $20. In fact, it turned out that the average price per barrel for 2004 was $38, representing a loss of $18 per barrel for the Congo. All in all, a shortfall of at least $504 million for 2004 alone - that's 20 times development aid for the same year!

The system of pre-sales for more than one year was abolished in 2005; however, three-month pre-sales are still practiced today, resulting in regrettable loss of earnings for producing countries.

Conclusion/Action: The trend towards transforming crude oil into a financial product is dangerous in many ways. While oil

---

40. WTI (West Texas Intermediate) benchmark oil.

extraction entails real risks for the vital and productive environment of many populations, while it necessarily diminishes their capital buried in the ground, while this extraction offers them no employment, these shares are transformed into financial products which escape them even more. For a long time, the countries where oil was extracted had to go into debt - notably through civil war - in order to transform financial debts into barrels of oil. These were the famous "oil-backed debts", whereby today's debts were secured by tomorrow's oil production. Today, other methods prevail. Part of the companies' profits come from the devaluation of oil from producing countries, and part from the difference between the price of crude forecast by institutes such as the IEA and the price of crude finally established on the spot market. We therefore need to provide instruments for renegotiating contracts in the event of major errors on the part of companies and/or fore-casting institutes.

Because beyond what we've described, the game between oil companies and the govern-ments of oil-producing countries isn't always a win-lose one. Sometimes it's a win-win game, because the players agree to share the wealth of the planet's soil, to the detriment of its true owners: the inhabitants (present and future), especially those closest to the extraction zones. Today in the Congo, despite production exceeding 110 million barrels a year, 70% of the population lives on less than $1 a day, half have no access to drinking water, and infant mortality is abnormally high.

We must therefore ensure that the largest possible share of oil extraction revenues is returned to the producing countries, and that it is put to the best possible use for their development, because once extracted, this wealth will no longer exist. The transformation of oil into a financial product makes this monitoring more difficult.

Conclusion

All this has to stop. For too long, oil companies have been taking advantage of the fragile institutions of heavily indebted poor countries to obtain oil at lower prices, thanks to the manipulation of information and collusion between companies.

At the start of their oil history, many African countries were dubbed the "new Kuwait", but some, after 40 years of oil production, still have a majority of their population living on less than $1 a day. The main cause of this poverty is certainly bad governance; but the disadvantageous sharing of oil wealth imposed by the companies has only served to destabilize already fragile economies. This is no longer tolerable, and we are all concerned, because let's not forget: the places where oil is consumed are often far from the places where it is extracted. We need to be aware of this: an African consumes 10 to 15 times less oil than someone living in the North. By accommodating ourselves to the practices of the oil companies, we are in a way accepting that the countries of Africa should pay for our dependence on black gold.

It's also worth remembering that not a single euro, not a single cent left to oil companies, benefits employment in developed countries, nor the effort to emerge from the crisis. It is no longer acceptable in a developed country for a company making billions in profits to abandon some of its employees to the hazardous dictates of the markets. Today, in the refining sector, tens of thousands of families are living in anguish. Those who argue in favor of refinery closures on the grounds of economic logic are either dishonest or incompetent, for as we have seen, despite profits driven by price effects, the companies have not made the necessary investments in the sector. This is unacceptable from an ethical point of view, and dangerous from a practical point of view, because France needs its refineries. The latest refinery strikes in October 2010, which left

2,600 service stations running dry in less than 6 days, showed us this.

Clearly, we can't expect oil companies to change their behavior on their own. As we've seen with the passing-on of gasoline prices, they don't even respect their commitments to the government. All that's left is legitimate constraint. But it is through vigilance and collective denunciation that the government will agree to take the necessary measures so that, at last, in the 21st century, we can hope for a better distribution of oil wealth.

Table of Contents

Introduction 7

1st Controversy: Oil Company Profits
Driven more by Higher Oil Prices than by
Increased Production 13

2nd Controversy: Oil Companies add more
Profits on the Backs of Consumers 19

3rd Controversy: How Companies Scuttle
their Own Refineries 27

4th Controversy: Oil Companies Pay no
Taxes in their own Countries, Nor in
Oil-Producing Countries. 35

5th Controversy: Oil Companies Deliberately
Undervalue Deposits in Oil-Producing
Countries 41

6th Controversy: Oil Companies Collude to
Buy up Deposits More Cheaply 51

7th Controversy: Oil Companies do not
Share Revenues Equitably with Producing
Countries 59

8th Controversy: How Companies Eat into
the Profits of Producing Countries 67

Conclusion 75

Best sellers Max Milo Editions

Hitler's banker, Jean-François Bouchard

Confessions of a forger, Éric Piedoie Le Tiec

The Koran and the flesh, Ludovic-Mohamed Zahed

Governing by fake news, Jacques Baud

Governing by chaos, Collectif

A political history of food, Paul Ariès

Mad in U.S.A.: The ravages of the "American model",
Michel Desmurget

Mondial soccer club geopolitics, Kévin Veyssière

Putin: Game master?, Jacques Braud

Treatise on the three impostors: Moses, Jesus, Muhammad,
The Spirit of Spinoza

TV Lobotomy, Michel Desmurget